The Armed Man:
A Mass For Peace
(choral suite)

Kyrie · Sanctus · Benedictus · Agnus Dei · Hymn Before Action

vocal score
SATB and piano/organ

Boosey & Hawkes Music Publishers Ltd
www.boosey.com

A vocal score for the complete *The Armed Man: A Mass for Peace* is also available (ISMN 979-0-060-11545-5). Full score and orchestral parts are available for hire from Boosey & Hawkes. Visit www.boosey.com for further information.

Note: Rehearsal letters in this choral suite correspond to those of the complete full score and orchestral parts. Bar numbers relate only to this choral suite.

Published by Boosey & Hawkes Music Publishers Ltd
Aldwych House
71–91 Aldwych
London
WC2B 4HN

www.boosey.com

ISMN 979-0-060-11410-6

Reprinted with corrections 2009

Printed in England by The Halstan Printing Group, Amersham, Bucks
Images courtesy of Virgin Records Ltd. Karl Jenkins photographed by Mitch Jenkins
Music setting by Andrew Jones

CONTENTS

The complete work, *The Armed Man: A Mass For Peace* is available on Virgin Venture Catalogue no: CDVE956

The CD features Karl Jenkins conducting The London Philharmonic Orchestra, The National Youth Choir of Great Britain with soloists Tristan Hambleton (treble), Mohammed Gad (Muezzin) and BBC Young Musician Of The Year 2000, Guy Johnston (cello).

The poignancy and relevance of the work is heightened by the fact that the CD was released on 10 September 2001, the day before the tragic events in the United States.

For further information, visit www.karljenkins.com

THE ARMED MAN:

A Mass For Peace

KARL JENKINS

Kyrie

2

4

8

10

Sanctus

16

24

Benedictus

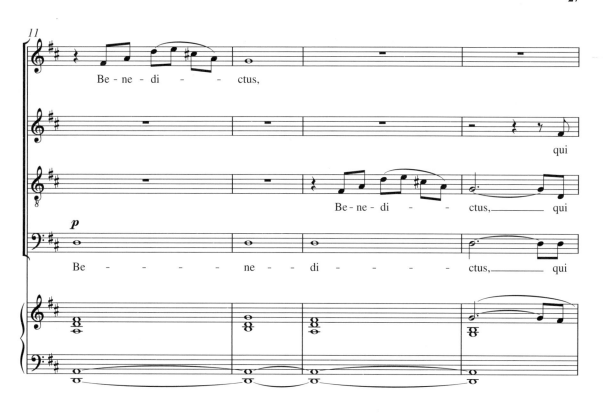

Agnus Dei

32

Hymn Before Action

Text: Rudyard Kipling

High lust and for-ward bear - ing, proud heart re-bel -lious brow,

High lust and for-ward bear - ing, proud heart re-bel -lious brow,

High lust and for-ward bear - ing, proud heart re-bel -lious brow,

High lust and for-ward bear - ing, proud heart re-bel -lious brow,